Why Didn't the DINOSAUR Cross the Road?

and Other Prehistoric Riddles

Joanne E. Bernstein and Paul Cohen

Pictures by Carl Whiting

ALBERT WHITMAN & COMPANY, Niles, Illinois

Also by Joanne E. Bernstein and Paul Cohen

Creepy Crawly Critter Riddles

Dizzy Doctor Riddles

Grand-Slam Riddles

Happy Holiday Riddles to You!

More Unidentified Flying Riddles

Riddles to Take on Vacation

Sporty Riddles

Touchdown Riddles

Unidentified Flying Riddles

What Was the Wicked Witch's Real Name?
and Other Character Riddles

Library of Congress Cataloging-in-Publication Data

Bernstein, Joanne E.
   Why didn't the dinosaur cross the road? and other prehistoric
riddles/Joanne E. Bernstein and Paul Cohen; illustrated by Carl
Whiting.
      p.   cm.
   Summary: A collection of riddles about dinosaurs and cave men,
including "What does a dinosaur have on the bathroom floor?
Rep-tiles."
   ISBN 0-8075-9077-0
   1. Riddles, Juvenile.   2. Dinosaurs—Humor.   3. Wit and humor,
Juvenile.   I. Cohen, Paul, 1945-   II. Whiting, Carl, ill.   III. Title.
   [DNLM: 1. Dinosaurs—Wit and humor.   2. Man, Prehistoric—Wit
and humor.   3. Riddles.]   90-12726
PN6371.5.B444   1990   CIP
818'.5402—dc20   AC

Dinosaur Data

Why didn't the dinosaur cross the road?
There were no roads.

How do baby dinosaurs hatch?
They eggs-it.

What does a dinosaur have on the bathroom floor?
Rep-tiles.

Can a lizard explode?
A dino-might.

How do dinosaurs see who's strongest?
They armor wrestle.

What do dinosaurs use for money?
Swamp-um.

What do you call a rhymin', jivin' dinosaur?
A rap-tile.

Why do prehistoric reptiles like shopping malls?
There are so many dino-stores.

At what age do dinosaurs die?
The Ice Age.

Pre-Hysteric Times

When the winged reptiles ruled, why were the other animals afraid?
It was the Age of Ptera.

Why were dinosaurs so calm?
They lived in pre-hysteric times.

What ancient people were attracted to black birds?
Cro-magnets.

Which prehistoric animals rarely told the truth?
Am-fib-ians.

How do we know that the dinosaurs enjoyed the glaciers?
An ice time was had by all.

How did dinosaurs improve their skin during the Ice Age?
Glacial cream.

What prehistoric cat are scientists always looking for?
The missing lynx.

What prehistoric cat refused to drink alcohol?
The sober-toothed tiger.

What was the most expensive prehistoric delicacy?
Cave-iar.

Dinosaurs from Head to Tail

Which prehistoric animal kept the warmest?
The woolly mammoth.

Why were the woolly mammoth's tusks so dirty?
There was no Ivory soap.

What prehistoric animal had the largest dental bill?
The woolly mam-mouth.

What do you call a mother brontosaurus?
Maxi-mum.

How many books do you read to a brontosaurus?
Two — he's a two-story dinosaur.

What's another name for Chinese brontosaurus stew?
One-ton soup.

Who wasn't as good as the new, improved brontosaurus?
Bront-X.

What do you get when you cross frogs with dinosaurs?
Leaping lizards.

Why does corythosaurus have the cleanest teeth?
He uses his crest.

Why would you laugh at sea serpents?
Because they're so finny.

What would tyrannosaurus do if he came upon some lions?
He'd have to swallow his pride.

What does tyrannosaurus do with cable wire?
She uses it as dental floss.

What is tyrannosaurus's favorite shape?
Rextangular.

Which dinosaur had three horns and three wheels?
Tri-cycle-tops.

Why is ankylosaurus a good dinner guest?
She brings her own plates.

How do flesh-eating dinosaurs recognize each other?
It takes one to gnaw one.

What kind of stories does diplodocus like?
Tall tails.

Which dinosaur did best in school?
The brain-tosaurus.

Which dinosaur failed everything but gym?
The brawn-tosaurus.

What dinosaur knew the most words?
The the-saurus.

Old Folks at Home

What's a cave kid's favorite food?
A club sandwich.

What's a cave kid's favorite toy?
Dino-riders.

What kind of dishes did cave people use?
Stoneware.

How did the cave detective solve cases?
By leaving no stone unturned.

Why couldn't the caveman pay his bills?
He was stone broke.

How close did cave people live to each other?
Just a stone's throw.

Why were cave dwellers cold at night?
They slept on bareskins.

Why did cave folks have wrinkled clothing?
It wasn't the Iron Age yet.

How did cave people like their sodas?
On the rocks.

Why was the small rock braver than the big rock?
He was a little boulder.

What salad dressing did cave people like?
Rock-fort.

What do cave people put on their bagels?
Cream cheese and rocks.

Where do cave people keep their weapons?
At the clubhouse.

How did cave artists tell the future?
The handwriting was on the wall.

What do you call a wandering cave person?
Meanderthal.

What was the most famous cave-age band?
The Rolling Stones.

What kind of protests did they have at Stone Age University?
Cave-ins.

How did the police force the end of the Stone Age?
They began the Copper Age.

Dig It

What kind of rock do you find fossils in, Sherlock?
Sedimentary, my dear Watson, sedimentary.

What did the angry archaeologist say to his student?
"I have a bone to pick with you."

What did the hip student reply?
"I can dig that."

What did the archaeologist sing when she was far
away from her digs?
My bone-y lies over the ocean.

What do you call a scientist who digs for ancient
comic books?
An Archie-ologist.

Dino-mite Careers

What can a dinosaur pianist play?
Nothing but scales.

Why do stegosauruses often make the track team?
They have spikes.

Why do some people think dinosaurs make good hit-men?
They are thought to be cold-blooded.

What do you call a dinosaur who wants to go to Yale?
A reppy.

Why were prehistoric dentists so successful?
There were lots of cave-ities to fill.

Why is triceratops a good taxi driver?
He has three horns.

Lizard Line-up

Who *is* supersaurus, really?
Clark Kent-osaurus.

Which dinosaur always comes in third in the
Olympics?
The bronze-osaurus.

Who was a famous flying mastodon?
Dumbo-saurus.

Who is the reptile queen of England?
A-lizard-beth II.

Who is her heir?
Bony Prince Charles.

And her daughter-in-law?
The Princess Di-no.

Why are English dinosaurs so wealthy?
They're never short of pounds.

What did they say when the first dinosaur flew an airplane?
Dino-soar!

What did they say when he crashed to the ground?
Dino-sore!

Who brought ptera-stroika to the Soviet reptiles?
Dino-saurbachev.

Ancient Antics

How do you stay on the good side of a fierce dinosaur?
Politely say "Allo, saurus" and run!

Why don't people buy dinosaur eggs?
Because they're egg-stinct.

What music style do you get when you cross a dinosaur with steel?
Heavy metal.

How do you get paint off dinosaurs?
Use serpentine.

What do you find in dinosaur junkyards?
Tyrannosaurus wrecks.

Who stars in dinosaur nightmares?
The boggy man.

What do you call twenty brachiosauruses?
A dino-score.

What do dinosaurs have in common with our riddles?
There are no more.

Paul Cohen and *Joanne Bernstein* go back a long way together. Their first riddle book was about amphibians, and now they've moved up the animal kingdom to reptiles. Who knows what will evolve next? When they're not thinking up riddles, Joanne teaches education in college, and Paul teaches chemistry in high school. They both live in Brooklyn, New York.

Carl Whiting is an illustrator and kindergarten teacher who lives in Evanston, Illinois. He enjoys working with children and is currently studying for his master's degree in early childhood education. Carl's hobbies include drawing and bicycling.